# STAFF INDUCTION

# STAFF INDUCTION

*A Practical Guide*

*Paul Davis*

*The Industrial Society*

First published in 1994 by
The Industrial Society
Robert Hyde House
48 Bryanston Square
London W1H 7LN
Telephone: 0171 262 2401

© *The Industrial Society 1994*
Reprinted 1995

ISBN 0 85290 883 0

**British Library Cataloguing-in-Publication Data**
**A catalogue record for this book is available from the**
**British Library.**

Typeset by: Photoprint, Torquay
Printed by: Hobbs The Printers, Southampton

Text illustrations: Sophie Grillet

The Industrial Society is a Registered Charity No. 290003

# Acknowledgements

Particular thanks to Jacquie Bambrough and my Industrial Society colleagues Julie Amber, Robin Bowden and Jo Gardiner for their help and support.

# Contents

# Introduction

The challenges we all face at work have never been greater.

- The challenges of coping with radical change and organisational restructuring.
- The challenge of working towards Total Quality.
- The challenge of adapting to new working patterns.

Successful organisations understand the importance of effective induction training in meeting these challenges.

Never has there been a greater need for effective induction schemes to help new employees contribute to the business more quickly. Never has there been such a need to help existing employees 're-orientate' themselves, after major structural and cultural change.

The common theme amongst best-practice organisations

and the vital *success factor* for any induction process, is that INDUCTION SHOULD BE EMPLOYEE CENTRED.

# Employee Centred Approach

The traditional approach to induction has often been 'organisation centred'. Induction in these circumstances has been little more than an 'information dump' about the products, services and basic amenities of the organisation. The move to an approach based around the individual has a number of implications:

First, as much as is possible, each individual should have a *personalised induction programme*.

Second, if induction training is truly employee centred, then it must contain elements of *activity, recognition, fun,* and *teamworking*.

Finally, the induction process should contain opportunities for individual discussion and feedback, through *regular review* and *target setting meetings*.

Through induction a new employee should become involved and productive, in the shortest time. We are not going to achieve this through an uninspiring 'information dump'. We may however, encourage LOYALTY, FLEX-IBILITY and UNCOVER NEW TALENT if our induction processes are developed around LEADERSHIP, MOTIVA-TION, INDIVIDUAL RESPONSIBILITY AND A CLEAR VISION OF COMMON PURPOSE.

# The Importance of a Good Induction Process

## Best Practice

Induction represents the start of many good practices in organisations. It establishes the framework for good employee involvement, good equal opportunities and effective training and development. Your organisation can demonstrate respect for the individual by the provision of induction programmes relevant to employees' particular needs and experiences.

## Organisational Benefits

When new employees' needs are met, your organisation will avoid the costly consequences of insufficient or inadequate induction training such as: high staff turnover, low productivity and poor quality outputs from new starters. New staff will:

- stay longer with your organisation.
- have a clear understanding of their role within it.
- be able to contribute to its success more quickly.

# Competitive Edge

Today the need for a good induction process is a core requirement of many workplace standards and employment legislation. Bodies concerned with best practice standards, such as Investors In People, will seek proof of induction material by your employees. This means that for your scheme to be effective it should provide opportunities for testing people's knowledge throughout the process.

In an increasingly competitive environment in many sectors of work, it becomes even more important to look for maximum effectiveness from employees in the shortest time. You can do this by designing an induction process that:

- motivates employees.
- builds confidence in employees.
- enables employees at every level to make their own decisions.

# Summary

- *Effective induction is important to your organisation's success, through the motivation and retention of new staff.*

■ *Every new employee should be entitled to a relevant, personalised induction programme.*

■ *Induction programmes should be focused on learning and attitude development, not just information giving. This will ensure your organisation matches the needs of statutory legislation and best practice standards, and secures competitive advantage.*

# Characteristics of Successful Induction Schemes

Some common themes emerge when you examine the induction processes of best practice organizations, from all sectors of work. The elements are:

- Programmes are based on the BUSINESS NEEDS of the organisation.
- They are MOTIVATIONAL.
- They are CUSTOMER OR CLIENT FOCUSED.
- They are concerned with QUALITY in delivery of service or product.
- Programmes establish a basis for EQUAL OPPOR-TUNITY and development.

In order to maximise these characteristics in the design of your programme, a number of actions need to be taken.

# Business Needs

Three main areas of effort will ensure that an induction process meets the needs of your organisation. First, needs change and therefore the induction process must be regularly reviewed to mirror these changes. Second, new employees require a clear definition of the mission of the organisation. The most effective way to achieve this is for senior managers to play a significant role in the induction process. Finally, induction training needs to be evaluated systematically in order to ensure it has met the business needs. The most comprehensive view of this is obtained by using the 'Endless Belt' of induction training (Figure 2.1) and assigning measures at each stage of this cycle.

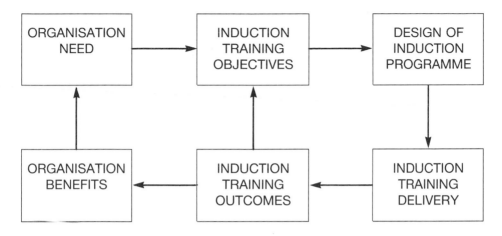

Fig. 2.1   The 'Endless Belt' of induction training.

# Motivation

It is difficult to meet business objectives with high absenteeism and staff turnover; therefore you must make motivation a core element of your programme. The major implication is that line manager involvement is paramount at all stages of the induction process. A further implication is that in induction training you must give as much emphasis to attitude development as to improvement of inductees' skills and enhancement of their knowledge of your product, service or environment.

# Customer and Client Focus

The earlier in your induction process that inductees develop a clear idea of customer or client needs, the quicker they are able to contribute to your organisation. This is particularly important in two areas: first, for employees who will be buffered from direct customer contact in their working role; second, for employees from sectors where the customer relationships are more complex, such as education, health and public sectors. One of the most effective ways to focus employees on to client needs is to involve customers in the delivery of induction training.

# Quality

An induction programme that helps your employees identify internal customers and their needs is vital for you to achieve quality in delivery of your product or service. Include elements in your programme that expose inductees to the maximum number, and variety, of staff. Give them the opportunity to discuss work informally, or more formally through the use of objective support grids (Figure 2.2). Emphasise the value of teamwork throughout the induction process.

# Equal Opportunities

Through teamworking people develop respect for each other. It is therefore particularly important to continue this process during induction. The commitment of your organisation to equal opportunities will be shown through the resources and effort given to every individual's induction. When organising group induction events you should make no distinction between employees, other than for technical training. Removing barriers to learning, and recognising the value of each person, are characteristics common to the managements of the most successful organisations.

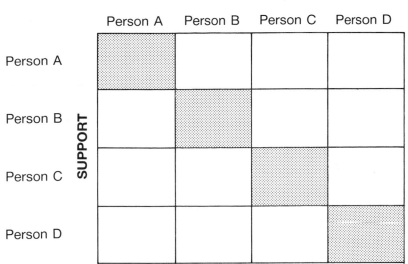

1. Work out your own objectives over the next period (1 year etc.).
2. Explain these to other people.
3. Agree the support needed from these colleagues.
4. Quid pro quo – colleagues explain their objectives to you, work out support required etc.

(Objectives are entered in tinted boxes. Support is entered in clear boxes).

5. Resolve incompatible objectives or duplicated support – or refer to next level of management if necessary.
6. Review progress jointly; learn lessons; repeat process.

Fig. 2.2   The Objectives/Support Grid.

# Summary

*Successful induction training, in any sector of work, should be concerned with:*

■ *business needs, and therefore should be systematically eva-luated and regularly updated.*

- *motivating employees to show that the role of the line manager in the induction process is fundamental not peripheral.*
- *providing customer focus, achieved by involving clients in the design and delivery of the programme.*
- *promoting quality and teamworking from the outset of a new employee's career.*
- *ensuring equal opportunity to unlock the full talents of all employees.*

# 3

# Whose Responsibility is Induction?

The word *induction* has its roots in the Latin word meaning *to lead to* or *to bring in*. The basis of successful induction is understanding that INDUCTION IS THE RESPONSIBILITY OF THE IMMEDIATE MANAGER OF THE NEW EMPLOYEE.

This must be at the core of any approach you adopt, although there are a number of other 'investors' who play a significant role.

In your organisation the 'investors' in the induction process would be some, or all, of the following:

■ The immediate manager of the inductee.

- The inductee.
- The members of the inductee's new team.
- The personnel or training team.
- The 'buddy' or peer from the team.
- The senior line manager.
- The union representative.
- The tutors used in group induction events.

It will be useful to consider the role of these investors and suggest various actions that each may like to take.

## The Immediate Manager of the Inductee

When accountability for induction lies with the immediate manager of the new employee, a number of good practices are made easier. First, leaders are in a far better position than others to identify induction training needs. This will come from their discussions with inductees during the recruitment process. They may also have some opportunity to assess the learning styles of new employees. Consequently line managers are able to combine this information with their own knowledge of the job and design a relevant and personalised induction process.

The actions that leaders must take in managing the induction process of an individual can be represented on the Action Centred Leadership model of John Adair (Figure 3.1). This ensures a balanced approach that meets the needs of the organisation and the individual. The model has been used to structure some of the most successful induction processes in a variety of organisations.

In order for inductees to gain maximum benefit from the induction process they must have the opportunity to

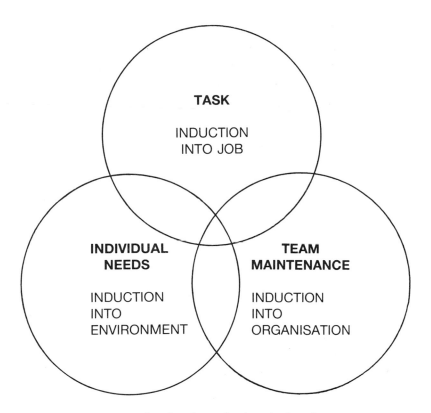

Fig. 3.1   Actions for leaders during induction.

discuss progress with their line manager. These reviews should be frequent in the early stages and establish targets specific to the individual (Figure 3.2). In the latter part of induction, this routine should form the basis at regular review and appraisal drills which exist in many organisations.

The role of the line manager is therefore:

■   To be accountable for the induction of any new member of their immediate team.

- To provide a personalised and balanced induction plan, based on the needs of the job, organisation and individual.
- To monitor and support the progress of the inductee, through regular reviews and target setting meetings.

## The Inductee

The more 'learner' driven the induction process, the more successful and rapid it will be. Stress is reduced by the control and flexibility that this approach allows the inductee. Consequently conditions for learning are improved.

Group induction training is not always possible and therefore resources for individual learning are important. Programmed Learning through the use of printed workbooks or computer-based methods, allows learning to take place at a pace suited to individual needs. Individual assignments and projects are powerful learning tools, although they must be handled sensitively and monitored closely. These 'learner led' methods may form a major part of induction training where work patterns allow little else.

Some inductees, particularly new senior managers or 'returners', maximise their induction training through Learning Networks. The benefits of being able to compare and contrast new experiences with peers is immense. Often the networks include peers from both within and outside the organisation.

Finally, it is important that inductees keep Induction Logs, to use as a basis for coaching and target setting discussions with line managers. These logs may be structured around Personal Development Plans that will be carried through

**TARGET SETTING SHEET**

NAME | Andrew Armstrong

PERIOD | from          to

*Achievements since last review*
Completed tutorial on software package and prepared a document.
Shadowed sales manager for one day and visited trade exhibition.
Attended product training course.

| *Target* | *Priority* | *Criteria* | *Comment* |
|---|---|---|---|
| Improve knowledge of competitors | 1 | Keep an updated file of data sheets | Use material from exhibition |
| Develop [French] language skills | 3 | Learn 10 new business terms per week | |

Manager's checklist for interview

1. Conditions
   Allocate sufficient time for the interview, 30–45 minutes.
   Ensure there will be no interruptions at all, except for safety emergencies.
   Ensure privacy.

2. Preparation for interview
   Keep to schedule of dates agreed with inductee.
   Help the inductee prepare for these reviews with self assessment sheets.
   Discuss inductees progress with other 'investors'.

3. The meeting
   Spend the time approximately as follows:–
   – One third of the time on the inductee's points and issues.
   – One third of the time on progress and achievements.
   – One third of the time setting new individual targets in line with the main induction programme.

4. After the meeting
   Ensure the inductee has a copy of the agreed targets.
   Ensure your manager receives a copy also, to gain support.

Fig. 3.2   Example of induction target setting sheet.

into their work role. The logs ensure a systematic record is kept of all learning experiences relevant to their induction.

The role of inductees is therefore:

- To take responsibility for their learning.
- To make use of the widest variety of learning opportunities, particularly those that they can control and which give them flexibility.
- To develop networks of people that can support them through their induction process.
- To be responsible for keeping records which will help them prepare for reviews.

## The Team Members

Team members can do much to speed the induction of a new employee. Simple actions such as the wearing of name badges by team members during the induction period, create a supportive environment. In these conditions an inductee can flourish and contribute more quickly to the team. It is important that team members are aware of a new starter's induction programme and, where possible, are involved in its delivery.

## The Personnel and Training Function

Two misconceptions about induction occur in many organisations. First, induction is seen as the sole responsibility of the Personnel or Training function. This is clearly not the case, as we have identified already that there are a number of other important investors in the process. Second, at the beginning of induction, sole responsibility lies with these central functions, and there is a transfer of responsibility, throughout the process, to the line manager. This is not the

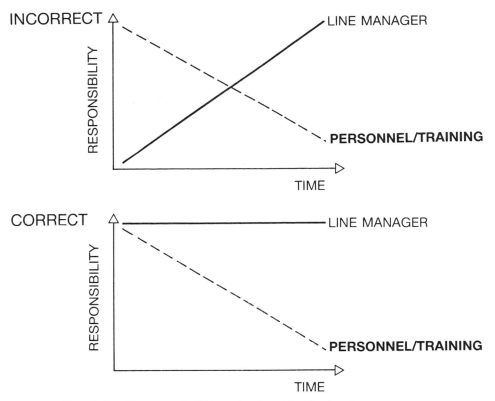

Fig. 3.3   Responsibilities during the induction process.

case, ACCOUNTABILITY FOR INDUCTION MUST ALWAYS LIE WITH THE IMMEDIATE MANAGER OF THE NEW EMPLOYEE. This concept is the key to successful induction (Figure 3.3).

The role of Personnel and Training staff in induction is one of assisting with a process that is essentially controlled by the various line managers in an organisation. Some of the tasks they may be 'contracted' to carry out would be:

■   Managing and coordinating group induction events.

- Advising line managers on the design of programmes that conform to the learning style of the inductees, best practice and current employment legislation.
- Producing induction training resources for individual or group use.

It is important that there is an overview of the process. Therefore the responsibility for evaluating the effectiveness of induction training should lie with these corporate functions.

## The 'Buddy' or Peer Role

The need for an assigned 'buddy' or peer group member to help with induction is well recognised in some sectors of work. Their role is to help inductees understand the detail and unwritten rules of their new work environment. It is important that the leader of the team fully briefs and trains the 'buddy' for this task.

A prime role of the 'buddy' may be to provide 'on the job' training. Where simple tasks are involved it would be useful for the buddy to be trained in job instruction. This would help them train inductees in a staged, systematic manner.

It is often useful to ask employees, who are relatively new themselves, to perform this role. They will be able to empathise with the concerns of the new starter. They are also best able to guide the new employee through the behavioural codes that exist in any work situation.

## The Senior Line Manager

One common characteristic amongst successful organisa- tions is the high level of involvement of senior managers in

the induction training. There are three main benefits resulting from this: First, they are able to offer a vision of the purpose and mission of the organisation. More importantly though they have the opportunity to check understanding, by questioning inductees face to face. Second, senior managers are able to reinforce the role of the inductees' line leaders by demonstrating commitment to them. Finally, they can gain valuable insight into their organisations by listening to inductees' comments and fresh ideas.

In some of the more successful organisations senior managers demonstrate their commitment by mentoring new staff. For the new employee this means that there is someone other than their line manager, who has an active role in their development. This process must be handled sensitively and only taken on by experienced senior managers, not necessarily from the same function or background as the inductee.

## The Representative

Where unions are recognised, representatives have a number of roles during the induction process. They can do much to emphasise the common aims of the organisation in seeking success for the benefit of customers, clients, the community, individual employees and 'investors' in the widest sense. They can explain their role in seeking protection and fairness for employees. Also they should be involved in delivering joint training on quality and other issues. Finally, representatives have a particular, often confidential, role of helping new employees through worries and problems concerned with induction.

## The Specialist Tutor

In most organisations group training events form part of the induction process for new employees. Existing staff from across the organisation are called upon to deliver group training related to their specialism. Rarely is the selection, briefing and training of these tutors sufficient, except in the best organisations. It is vital that, where a number of specialist tutors are involved in group training of inductees, they present a uniform and coordinated message. Figure 3.4 outlines a suggested format for a training event designed to help tutors in their role.

# INDUCTION TUTORS' WORKSHOP

**One day event**

| | |
|---|---|
| **Course aim:** | To enable staff members with specialist roles to be able to deliver induction training to a group. |
| **Training outcomes:** | To be able to design an induction training session. To be able to manage a training session in a flexible manner. To be able to use appropriate listening, presentation, facilitating and questioning skills to optimise the learning opportunities for inductees. |

| | TOPIC | PURPOSE | ACTIVITY |
|---|---|---|---|
| **Session 1** | Mission and Vision | To establish a common purpose amongst tutors | Plenary session with a senior manager |
| **Session 2** | The Team | To create a team approach to ensure a consistent message | SWOT presentations by each tutor on themselves |
| **Session 3** | Listening skills | To practice listening skills in order to meet inductees' exact needs during training | Active listening exercises in pairs with plenary feedback |
| **Session 4** | Specifying Objectives | To enable tutors to understand the importance of training objectives | Presentation of case study by course leader followed by syndicate work and feedback |
| **Session 5** | Induction | To enable tutors to gain knowledge of the organisation's policy on induction | Lecture by course leader |
| **Session 6** | Skills for Induction Training | To practice skills appropriate to running group training sessions | Video and role play |
| **Session 7** | Action Session | To commit to practical actions | Facilitated discussion |

Fig. 3.4   Suggested training event for course tutors.

# Summary

- *The key to successful induction is that it is made THE RESPONSIBILITY OF THE IMMEDIATE MANAGER OF THE NEW EMPLOYEE.*

- *The **line manager** is responsible for preparing a personalised induction programme and reviewing progress with the inductee throughout the process.*

- *Other 'investors' have important roles in the induction process, for which they must be prepared.*

- *The **team members** should help the inductee contribute to the team as soon as possible.*

- *The **Personnel and Training** function role is to support line managers by providing induction training resources and events. They are also responsible for evaluating the training.*

- *The '**Buddy**' also has an important role in supporting the line manager, by providing on the job training and advice to the inductee.*

- *The task of **senior managers** is to provide a clear vision to people and show commitment by, for example, mentoring new employees.*

- ***Employee representatives** provide a vital source of support for new starters. Their role should extend across a wide variety of induction training topics.*

- ***Inductees** should take responsibility for their learning by using the widest possible variety of learning methods and opportunities.*

# Structure of the Induction Process

Effective induction is concerned with motivating people to become productive in the shortest time and to stay with your organisation. It is a leadership task. Therefore, it should be structured on models of motivation and leadership as described earlier, in order to make it wholly effective. One of the most helpful frameworks on which to structure your induction programmes is Maslow's Hierarchy of needs (Figure 4.1). This suggests a strategy for approaching the various issues and topics important to staff in new roles or jobs.

A comprehensive and successful scheme is one that meets the needs of an inductee as they progress into your organisation. Initially, inductees will want to know about their *individual* safety, security, health, comfort and

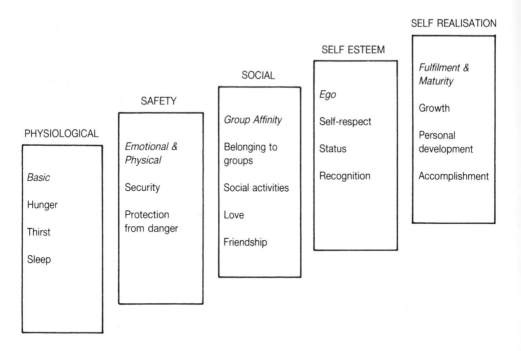

Fig. 4.1   Maslow's Hierarchy of Needs.

welfare. Subsequently they will be keen to understand the *tasks* and responsibilities expected of them. Finally they would want to see their role in a *team*, and how they can make a contribution to the organisation and its objectives.

It is useful to define the four stages of induction:

- Pre-employment
- Primary induction
- Main induction
- Review

In the *pre-employment* phase your programmes should be concerned with preparing inductees and their teams for induction. During *primary induction* your concern is to orientate employees and offer training to ensure their basic safety and well being. Information on the job, the organisation and the working environment will go into the main part of your induction process. The opportunity for inductees to be able to *review* their learning and understanding is essential. The latter stages of an induction programme should help employees incorporate the training into their work situation.

## Timing of Induction

The timing of these various phases is an important consideration. Learning and retention of information by inductees will be improved if induction is not crammed into the very early stages of the programme. Precise timings are very much dependent on the legislation and standards covering your occupation and organisation. Another factor may be the extent to which you can bring groups of new employees together. However there is some benefit in designing programmes that involve short, intensive learning opportunities over an extended period, interspersed with work experience.

# Pre-employment

The induction process begins during recruitment and selection. Many organisations lose a valuable opportunity to inform and involve staff in the period between the acceptance of job offer, and the start of employment. Those organisations that adopt a systematic approach to this phase benefit from the speed with which new employees become integrated into the organisation.

In order to make best use of this pre-employment period, your organisation should carry out a number of actions. Give the recruits publications, audio visual and reference material produced by your organisation. Make arrangements for these new starters to visit the workplace. Indeed, adopt any action that gives them confidence and the opportunity to identify how they can help your organisation at this early stage.

The printed or audio visual resources that you can provide fall into three categories:

### *Reference information* such as

- Organisation and accountability charts
- Terms and conditions
- Employee handbook [Appendix 1]
- Telephone list

The important points to remember about reference material are:

- Make items accessible and user friendly.
- Make someone responsible for updating the information.
- Make the material easy to update, e.g. looseleaf format for the staff handbook, computerised telephone lists.
- Clearly index the items.
- Name the originator of the material.
- Date the documents.

### *Working documents* such as

- Induction logs
- Induction workbooks or programmed learning texts
- Employee development manual

### *Supporting material*, for example

- Corporate presentations on video or audio cassette
- Employee reports
- House journals
- Recommended reading
- Press cuttings

Visiting the place of work before starting employment can allay many fears experienced by new employees. Visits act as dry runs for people to test travel options and to assess the provision of facilities that may be needed. They also enable new employees to meet their 'buddy' and other new team members. The value of these visits in helping the integration of new employees into your organisation should not be underestimated.

Pre-employment visits are of particular value to line managers. They provide opportunities for managers to identify any special training requirements that were not apparent during selection. They also provide time for leaders to understand the needs of new starters with disabilities. Arrangements can then be made before the start of employment.

It is clear that there are many learning opportunities that can be encouraged before the start of employment. It is very much a characteristic of more successful organisations that this period is used in a planned, creative and worthwhile way to the benefit of both employer and new starters. The more caring organisations go a stage further and become involved in *Pre-Recruitment* Training with great benefit to themselves and the community [see Appendix 2].

# Summary

- *Prepare a publication pack of printed and other material from your organisation for recruits to view before the start date.*
- *Encourage, where possible, pre-employment visits to the place of work to aid the integration of recruits into your existing teams.*

# Primary Induction

Initial or primary induction has two objectives. First, to orientate your new starters and second, to protect them in the work environment. By its very nature this phase of induction must take place **immediately** employees join the organisation. It must also cover all new employees, irrespective of their future role. Often there is a great temptation to overload employees with information in this initial period. This is counterproductive for two reasons: First, unless the information given relates to the inductees' immediate priorities, they will not be interested. Second, the stress and anxiety of people when starting a new role, affect their ability to understand and retain information. The material you offer must be directly related to your new employees' needs and priorities at this early stage.

## Orientating Inductees

Your immediate responsibility to your new employees is to provide information, in a systematic manner that relates to:

- their surroundings i.e. building/environment layout, access and exit points.
- their safety i.e. security precautions, first aid facilities, evacuation and other emergency procedures.
- their comfort i.e. toilet and hygiene facilities, private areas, rest and catering facilities.
- their timekeeping i.e. breaks, hours and working patterns.
- their colleagues, through introductions and informal meetings.

It will also be helpful to give an explanation of some of the terms, jargon and acronyms used in your organisation to help inductees make sense of the rest of the induction.

## Protecting Inductees

Another area that must be dealt with promptly is the protection of the employees and some of the relationships they will enter on joining your organisation. Most societies consider these issues vitally important and therefore many countries have established a statutory legal framework in which to work.

At this primary stage of induction you must explain:

- the relationship between employees and the *clients* or customers of your organisation. This may be covered in legislation and codes of practice specific to your sector, and may include agreements about the confidentiality of information.
- the relationship between you as the *employer,* and the new starters as employees. This relationship will be the subject of a contract of employment in which various individual and collective rights are protected, in Employment Acts.
- the responsibility of new employees to themselves and *other employees* in terms of health and safety. Increasingly, the influence of European Community Directives means that a wider range of health and safety issues than has been common practice in the United Kingdom in the past should be dealt with at induction.

The essential elements of these protections must be communicated at the very start of employment. This is to protect your organisation and new employees when they are most vulnerable. You must regularly update the information you deliver as new legislation comes into play.

Primary induction is therefore concerned with satisfying some of the basic needs of your new starters so that they are able to broaden their learning as early as possible. Some of these elements are covered by legislation, for example, safety. Training on these elements must in many cases be given immediately to all inductees. It is important to assess employees' understanding of the important issues raised in primary induction before proceeding to the next stage of induction.

# Summary

■ *Provide essential information immediately to inductees, concerning their safety and well-being. Check that they understand it.*

■ *Explain to inductees the contractual relationships they are entering into with the organisation, clients and other people.*

# Main Induction

It is important to have a clearly defined **induction policy** for your organisation that establishes:

– When programmes should be developed.
– Who is responsible.
– Standards, in terms of time periods, within which various stages should be completed.
– Criteria for the evaluation of induction training.

The main induction process in your organisation, the training methods you employ and the targets you adhere to, will be influenced by other factors in the absence of a policy.

In best practice organisations there is a high investment in this stage of the process, in terms of time and other resources. The benefits that derive from this investment are proven by commercial and other forms of success. The benefits also arise out of a broad approach to the main induction process based on an effective introduction into the work environment, the organisation and the job.

## Induction into the Work Environment

At induction there are a number of issues to be covered which centre around individual employees and their well-being. Some of the issues will have been addressed at the primary induction stage. In essence they fall into the category of health, safety and welfare of the individual. The well-being of the organisation depends on the well-being of the individual, and consequently, sufficient emphasis should be given to this part of the main induction process.

It is important to involve people concerned for the individual, such as union representatives and occupational health staff, in the design of this part of the programme. It is far more efficient to expend effort at induction, in 'preventative' training, than to deal with the consequences of some of the issues that may arise. You can help inductees in a new working environment by:

■ outlining the hazards that exist and offering training so that they can develop individual strategies to deal with them.

■ providing information on sensitive issues they may meet.

■ raising awareness of the support networks and services that they can call upon.

It is important that training is carried out by 'competent' people in partnership with your line managers. It is also important to ensure the training methods employed provide opportunities to monitor inductees' understanding. Positive attitudes and sound individual strategies for dealing with sensitive issues should be the aim of this type of training.

> **EXAMPLE**
>
> A large firm of solicitors offers training in assertiveness to all young inductees at an early stage of their induction. The training arose from a need to provide young employees with strategies to deal with harassment.

The value of a well prepared staff handbook (Appendix 1) that covers these individual issues is immense.

# Summary

- *Provide information and training on a broad range of issues to protect the individual in a new environment. The issues will broadly fall under the heading of health, safety and welfare.*
- *Provide 'preventative' training in a full range of health and safety issues relevant to the inductees' work environment.*
- *Involve union and occupational health staff and other competent personnel, concerned for the individual and the work environment.*

# Induction into the Organisation

Whether your organisation is a small charity employing a dozen people or a large, multinational corporation, employees in new roles will have the same needs for information about the organisation. They will want a map, a *framework*, a context for the organisation and its aims. They will want to know where they *fit in*. They will also want to know 'how things are done round here' i.e. the rules and the *culture*.

# Organisation Values and Direction

Most organisations, from whatever sector, will have a **mission statement**. This describes the aims and values of the organisation and needs to be explained to new employees. Many organisations will have developed departmental mission statements which make this process so much easier. Other important policies can be derived from statements.

---

**EXAMPLE**

A major power tool manufacturer was inundated with job applications when opening a new factory. They had publicised their induction policy and commitment to each individual's training and development as part of their recruitment campaign.

---

**Corporate videos** are an effective medium for describing the whole organisation and the relationships within it. They may be made to support the annual report, or specifically commissioned for induction training. Their advantage is that they are suitable for both group or individual, 'learner driven', training.

> ### EXAMPLE
>
> A major retailer has redesigned induction training around a set of workbooks and videos, followed by question-and-answer tutorials This has improved retention of information amongst new employees. The employees, many of whom are part-time, are able to learn at a pace and time that suits them individually.

The members of an inductee's new team can do much to put **business plans** into context. They can describe departmental action plans in relevant terms and outline their progress.

Progress towards targets and plans at the local level can be seen by the inductee in team briefings and similar **communication and involvement systems**. They will establish a view of the values of the organisation, on the actions and managerial responses seen in these processes. Much of an organisation's culture is established by the way employees particularly new ones are informed and consulted.

> ### EXAMPLE
>
> A successful pottery firm, renowned for innovation, tells inductees within the first half-hour of their first day about how the company will keep them informed, and how they value their ideas through the suggestion scheme.

Total Quality in the delivery of products or services is strived for in many organisations. As part of their induction into the organisation it is vital that staff receive training in Quality so that they may develop their own **individual plans**, at an early stage.

## Structure of the Organisation

Once an inductee has an understanding of the values and direction of an organisation they will want to know where *they fit* in to it. **Organisation charts** can do much to show the inductee some of the often complex, inter-relationships which exist. However they fail to bring out the accountabilities of each level. This is best done by means of **accountability charts** [see Appendix 3]. Therefore, each person entering a new role should be given the page or pages of the accountability chart that show where they fit in.

---

### EXAMPLE

A fast-growing restaurant chain encourages new starters to 'drive' their own induction programme. The inductees are issued with organisation and accountability charts and induction is then based around interviews, that they arrange, with people essential to their role. A mentor is assigned to support them in this process.

---

Relationships that exist outside the organisation are equally important for the inductee to understand. The delivery of most services and products depends on a chain of supply, involving a number of organisations and agencies. It is important that these organisations are part of the induction process for any individual.

> **EXAMPLE**
>
> A leading printing technology company adopts the prac-
> tice of involving the employees of its suppliers, distributors
> and customers, as *delegates*, on a major part of its own
> induction training courses. There are many benefits to this
> approach, not least improved teamworking across organ-
> isational boundaries.

## Culture

For people to work effectively in a new role they must have
an understanding of the *rules* and *culture* that govern their
working environment. The inductee's immediate leader can
be a role model, and do much to explain the relevance of
policies to the new starter. Other people also have
particular roles. The 'buddy' or 'starter's friend' is often the
best person to further clarify the rules of the organisation. A
senior manager or 'mentor', however, can best put the
culture of the organisation into context for the new
employee.

# Summary

■ *Give inductees a structured view of your organisation by
providing training based on:*

  *– your mission statement.*
  *– your business plans.*
  *– your communication and involvement systems.*

■ *Help them understand where they fit in by giving them:*

 *– an organisation chart.*
 *– their accountability charts.*
 *– opportunities to meet people important to their role both within and outside your organisation.*

■ *Help inductees understand the rules and culture of your organisation by:*

 *– publishing clear policies.*
 *– involving a variety of staff (line manager, peers, senior managers) to explain the formal and informal issues that they raise.*

# Induction into the Job

This is the most important part of the induction process for people in your organisation. Its purpose is to ensure employees have the information and particular skills to perform their new jobs effectively. This means they must have a clear definition of their *role* and the *standards* expected. They must have the *skills* and *resources* to carry out their tasks. Lastly they must understand the *importance* and *value* of their role in the organisation.

## Job Role

The immediate manager must discuss with the inductee individually the job and performance expected. A well written **job description** will help the manager define the main tasks and accountabilities. **Procedures** need to be explained as they affect the inductee, and understanding needs to be checked. Your area of work may require other information to be learnt at this stage as well.

---

**EXAMPLE**

A major lift engineering company prepares an inductor's pack for the line manager. This contains additional information to the inductee's pack. Both documents support induction in three areas: general induction, work induction and safety induction. This firmly sets responsibility for induction with the line manager.

---

## Standards

In almost all occupations standards of performance are defined. Managers must explain these standards to individual inductees and agree a series of targets with them, as they work towards these standards. Inductees also need to know what levels of performance they can expect from others.

## Resources

Ensuring new starters have access to the resources to do their jobs can be dealt with at a number of levels. It may mean significant training on equipment related to your sector of work. It could simply involve telling inductees how to obtain supplies of work materials. It could also mean ensuring they have the necessary language, or jargon, to operate effectively in the organisation.

> **EXAMPLE**
>
> New store staff joining one of the most successful retail chains receive a jargon handbook as part of their starter pack.

## Importance of the Job

The value and importance of the job must be emphasised to the person taking on the role. Senior managers, or indeed clients, should be involved in describing the effects of good or bad job performance to inductees. The inclusion of job rotation in an induction programme can also 'bring to life' the whole process in your organisation and the value of a particular job.

# Summary

*Help inductees to take on their new jobs by:*

- *Clearly defining their role through discussions on the job description and relevant procedures.*
- *Stating the standards of performance and agreeing targets towards them.*
- *Providing resources and technical training as appropriate, and making them aware of the value of their job.*

# Review of Induction

Much of the effort put into previous stages of your induction process will be wasted unless frequent reviews between inductees and their line managers are carried out. These reviews have a vital role in improving learning and retention of material. Not only is it an opportunity for your new employees to ask questions, but also a chance for leaders to help new employees translate their learning into the work situation. Information from these reviews should be collated to form part of the evaluation of induction training in your organisation.

# Summary

- *Reviews between the line manager and inductee should be seen as an integral part of any induction process.*
- *The purpose of the reviews is to:*

  - *Consolidate an inductee's learning.*
  - *Develop agreed targets for the inductee.*
  - *Gain information for the evaluation process.*

# Methods of Induction Training

There are many training and learning events which you can use to build an induction process for an individual. Successful organisations provide a wide range of resources for induction for three reasons:

1. Induction training is quicker and more effective when training is matched to people's learning styles.
2. A choice of methods allows employees to receive training and information at the correct time.
3. Programmes can be easily created to meet the special needs of some employees.

Listed below are some of the training and learning opportunities that can be used to create an effective staff induction programme. They can be classified as:

- individual study.
- group work.
- experience based methods.

# Individual Study

There are many benefits from providing resources for individual study as part of your induction process. For your inductees this will encourage a 'learner driven' approach, which often improves the retention and understanding of material. For your organisation, materials are developed which can be used flexibly perhaps in an open learning centre.

## Individual Study – Listening and Reading

Offer your inductees a structured reading programme. Alternatively, provide spoken material on audio cassette. Build in opportunities for their understanding to be checked by their manager or a competent person.

### Benefits

Using these materials learning can be at a time and a pace suited to the employee.

### Drawbacks

This type of training can be ineffective if not monitored and supported by line managers.

---

### EXAMPLE

A successful contract-catering organisation provides all new employees with a series of audio cassettes that cover general company information. Previously this part of induction was not given the emphasis it deserved. The company finds this media to be the most effective for its employees, in this multi-site operation.

---

## Individual Study – Programmed Learning

Programmed learning requires inductees to make responses to questions given in the training material. Two types of resource could be offered at induction:

### WORKBOOKS

#### Benefits of using workbooks for induction training:

- This training encourages people to think and anticipate their own responses in work situations.
- The workbooks are a basis for review and learning, through discussions with line managers and peers.

#### Drawbacks of using workbooks:

- This induction method is particularly suited to correct attitude development in customer/client facing jobs. It may be less appropriate for other roles.

> **EXAMPLE**
>
> A leading housing association uses workbooks in the induction training of part-time care workers. Workbooks are completed individually in stages, by new employees. Small group tutorials, involving other new employees and a supervisor, are then arranged periodically to review learning.

## COMPUTER BASED METHODS

Offer *computer based training, interactive video* or other *multimedia* methods of induction training.

### Benefits of computer based training methods:

- Immediate feedback is given to trainees' responses, improving learning.
- With computer based training, a tutor can support a greater number of inductees than in classroom based training.
- These induction training media can be accessed flexibly by teleworkers and other distant workers.
- It can be relatively low cost if a large number of new employees use this medium. Existing employees are able to use material for refresher training, if necessary.

### Drawbacks of computer based training methods:

- The programmes may not allow enough supplementary questioning by inductees which will inhibit their learning.
- Computer based methods may not be cost effective for induction training in certain organisations.

- Inductees, especially returners, may not be comfortable using computer based methods of training.
- These induction materials can be difficult to update to meet changing business needs.

# Group Work

Group work can be one of the most effective induction training methods. *Induction training events* can be arranged. These could involve lectures, discussions and case studies appropriate to your organisation. These activities provide many opportunities for learning to be consolidated, through questions, feedback and interaction with other inductees.

## Group Work – Induction Training Events

Organise formal induction courses where a number of people have a similar training requirement, for example, at the primary induction stage. Cover only a limited number of topics in the early stages. Consider short intensive sessions of say, two hours, over a six to eight-week period, instead of a crammed one or two-day course. Clarify the roles of those charged with providing these courses (Figures 5.1 and 5.2).

### Benefits of induction courses

- Inductees can make use of a variety of learning opportunities in group training events through listening, questioning and discussion.
- Information can be conveyed at the same time and in the same manner, to a number of people.

---

## INDUCTION COURSE – NOTES FOR TUTORS

### Preparation

■ Be clear about the purpose of your presentation. Check this with the course coordinator.

■ You will be part of a team of tutors. Find out the tutors before and after your session, find out their content and delivery methods and design your presentation accordingly.

■ If you only have a short session, do not underestimate the amount of time needed for proper preparation. It is often more difficult to cover material well in a short time. (It may take you four hours to prepare a 20 minute presentation, if it is new).

■ Provide clear, well prepared handout material to support your presentation. 10 summary points on a single sheet can be more effective than a mass of documents.

### Delivery

■ Do not be afraid to alter seating arrangements to match the purpose of your session. Different arrangements such as 'U shaped', 'Cabaret' or 'Classroom' style suit different purposes, such as 'involvement', 'discussion' or 'information giving' respectively.

■ Be familiar with the audio visual equipment you will use.

■ Avoid jargon or explain it fully, if you use it.

■ Remember how you would feel starting a new role or job. Do not overload inductees.

### Review

■ Build in opportunities to assess inductees' current knowledge at the beginning of your session, and check understanding throughout and at the end

---

Figure 5.1  Suggested notes for induction course tutors.

# INDUCTION COURSE – NOTES FOR ADMINISTRATOR

In administering an induction course you have three responsibilities:

Care of the inductees; Care of the tutors; Care of the practical arrangements.

## Inductees

■  Issue formal invitations to inductees and a map of the venue. Be clear about start and finish times and what materials they need to bring. Suggest an appropriate dress code.

■  Inform the inductee's managers of their attendance and send them a course programme so that they can discuss it.

■  Identify any special needs that inductees may have in a classroom situation, and plan for them.

## Tutors

■  Ensure tutors have a clear brief for their sessions.

■  Send them a programme and highlight the standards expected in terms of delivery and supporting documentation.

■  Clarify their equipment requirements and get the tutor to nominate a deputy who will cover in their absence.

■  Issue course assessment sheets to inductees and ensure that this feedback is given to tutors.

## Practical Arrangements

■  Help create an environment where inductees can concentrate on learning. Do this by reducing distractions for the group and helping individuals with their practical concerns such as transport.

Figure 5.2   Suggested notes for induction course administrators.

- This form of induction training can be very effective in helping attitude development of people in new roles.
- Skilled tutors can offer constructive feedback to inductees and check their understanding of material.

### Drawbacks of induction courses

- It is not always possible to pull people together in groups at the right time.
- If the course is simply a series of lectures, then no assessment of the level of understanding of the material by inductees is made.
- In a group situation some inductees may be inhibited from asking questions.
- Transition from a highly structured induction course in a classroom, to the real work environment, is sometimes difficult for inductees.

# Experience-based Methods

Some of your group induction training events should contain elements of experienced-based learning for inductees. These may be *visits* or *simulations* and *role plays*. Individual inductees may also benefit from structured *on the job training*, where the 'tutor' uses *job instruction* techniques or similar. 'Learning by doing' is probably the most powerful induction training method at your disposal, and should be included as much as possible in your staff induction programmes.

## Experience-based Methods – Visits

Organise structured visits and tours of your place of work or of other agencies or organisations, with which your inductees will be involved. Ensure that inductees are properly briefed on the processes and activities they will see on the visit.

### Benefits of structured visits

■ These learning events can be motivational for the new employee, as well as giving depth to information already received.

■ Inductees have an opportunity to consolidate their learning by speaking to a wide variety of employees.

■ Information is better retained by inductees as a result of these experiences.

### Drawbacks of Visits

■ If inductees are not adequately prepared for the visit nor debriefed following the visit, then much of the benefit of this training method is lost.

## Experience-based Methods – Simulations and Role Plays

Provide resources so that inductees can learn through 'acting out' scenarios in teams (simulations) or individually (role plays). Simulations involve responding to written scenarios and timed inputs by a trainer, where your inductees work as part of a team. In role plays, individual inductees try out their responses to given situations in a 'safe' environment.

### Benefits of simulations and role plays

■ Materials can be specifically designed for your work

amongst inductees, for example: assertiveness, leadership, problem solving and teamworking.

## Drawbacks of simulations and role plays

- These exercises often require long, continuous periods of time to run and review.
- The methods are heavily dependent on the tutor's skill in facilitating, feeding back to inductees and drawing out learning points.
- The written support materials need very detailed and careful preparation.
- Some inductees may feel uncomfortable when role playing and this may inhibit their ability to learn.

### Experience-based Methods – On the Job Training

Appoint some employees as 'tutors', to provide on the job training to individual inductees. Ensure that 'tutors' adopt a systematic approach, such as **job instruction** for simple tasks. Job instruction involves *assessing* an inductee's current knowledge of a task; *demonstrating* the task and checking the inductee's understanding at each step; letting the inductee *practice* the task to achieve a given standard; *monitoring* the inductee's progress to ensure the standard is maintained.

### Benefits of on the job training

■ On the job training is simple to operate and is seen as motivational by inductees.
■ Job instruction allows inductees to be assessed as competent for a task.

### Drawbacks of on the job training

■ The method is dependent on the technical and inter-personal skills of the tutor for it to be effective.

# Summary

■ *In order to ensure timely effective induction for all staff, develop a range of induction training methods.*
■ *Provide opportunities for individual study through:*
    *– written texts*
    *– workbooks*
    *– computer based training*
*that can be used flexibly but with opportunities for periodic reviews of learning with line managers and peers.*

■ *Arrange group induction training such as*

  *– lectures*

  *– discussions*

*but avoid overloading inductees during the early stages. Train the specialist 'tutors' or speakers. Be conscious of inductees' ability to learn, rather than the ease of administration of group events.*

■ *Include experience based training for individuals or groups through:*

  *– visits*

  *– business simulations or role plays*

  *– structured on the job training*

*to speed up induction by the use of these very active methods of learning.*

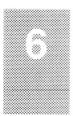

# When Should Induction Programmes Be Set Up?

Induction programmes should be designed to help your employees through change, so that they can be effective in the shortest possible time. The most obvious transition is that of recruit to employee. However, there are other changes that should trigger the setting up of induction programmes for one or a number of staff. These might be job changes; change in response to new technology or organisational change; change due to mergers and new alliances. Your organisation will benefit from adopting a broadly based and sympathetic approach to help employees through these changes.

## New Starters

When people join your organisation they will have some common requirements from the induction process. Also, certain groups of employees will have particular needs to be met. These needs may arise from the nature of their contract with your organisation, their special needs, or their recent background before joining you.

The variety of contracts that exist between new employees and employers is becoming increasingly diverse. Many employees have a temporary or 'contract' status. A growing number of jobs are now part-time.

## Temporary Staff

For temporary and contract staff, induction must provide a clear vision of the 'common purpose' of your organisation. This is best achieved by the involvement of senior managers in the induction of these staff. This is rarely carried out, except in the best practice organisations. An added benefit for senior management is the chance to hear about the perceptions of the organisation from this important group of people.

## Part-time Staff

Part-time staff need flexible induction programmes to fit in with their work patterns. For this process to be effective it is particularly important to assign a 'helper' or 'buddy' to the inductee. This helps to accelerate the part-timer's understanding of the organisation's culture. Otherwise this process may not be as quick as for full-time staff.

## Special Needs

New staff may have special needs from the induction process. It is very important that the person responsible for induction – the line manager – allots the time necessary to understand the exact needs of an inductee. People with disabilities will have special needs, as may secondees from other organisations or other branches of your own organisation. The key issue is to ensure that you make adequate preparations.

For people with disabilities this may involve extended visits to your place of work during the pre-employment stage. After discussions with inductees, facilities and support can then be in place at the start of employment. The design of any induction programme, and the training methods offered, should as always be specific to the individual.

The induction of long or short-term secondees into your organisation is particularly helped by the appointment of a helper or 'buddy'. They will be able to guide people through the new culture in the most efficient way. The level of training and preparation of existing staff to support inductees with special needs, often distinguishes the best practice organisations.

The recent background of people coming into your organisation may influence the needs they have from induction. Some examples might be young people coming from full-time education or people returning to work after an extended absence. Effective integration of these staff depends on helping them through this transition period and encouraging them to seek support from peers in the same situation.

## Young People

The induction process is particularly important for young people so that they can become motivated and productive as soon as possible. Programmes for young people should be practical, systematic and include regular opportunities for reviews. In the best practice organisations, these programmes are set in the context of an overall policy for the development of young employees.

Your induction programmes for young people should include a high level of practical experience-based learning. Structured visits to agencies and organisations with which you work, are immensely useful. As always, records of all induction training activities should be kept in an induction log.

It is particularly important that induction programmes for young people are well structured with opportunities for regular feedback. Careful planning will be needed to ensure inductees are employed on worthwhile and varied tasks throughout this process. Regular feedback and frequent progress reviews are also vital to motivate young people through their induction. Formal progress reviews should take place every three months for young employees in the first three years of their employment.

## Development Training

An important characteristic of the most successful organisations is that they establish an explicit contract with their young employees, to govern both induction and early training. Employers guarantee to provide special services, such as newsletters, social gatherings and the opportunity to take part in community projects. Together with training in job related skills, this process is called *development training*. It is designed to help form attitudes in a positive way.

Other elements included in development training are:

■ vocational skills training towards qualifications.
■ a residential or outdoor experience such as Outward Bound, or the Industrial Society's 'Responsibility at Work' conferences.
■ practical training in leadership and communication skills.
■ health awareness training and fitness programmes.
■ youth forums, where young employees question senior management and union representatives.
■ further education.
■ employee volunteering.

## Returners

When people are returning to work there are a number of needs that must be met during induction. The induction process should include tasks that allow the returner to practice skills and regain previous standards of performance. Depending on your work sector, new equipment and technologies need to be explained, as the pace of development is increasingly fast. Less obvious issues for returners which may need to be addressed are confidence building and acceptance by others. Opportunities in the induction process to receive feedback from the line manager are therefore vitally important.

## Job Changes

When people change jobs within your organisation, an induction programme needs to be provided. As employees move to different management levels or new job roles across the organisation they encounter very different working environments. Sadly, induction programmes are rarely initiated in these circumstances and the effectiveness of the individual and organisation are reduced. By providing induction you will make the employee's transition a smooth process. The investment will be more than repaid in terms of productivity and speed of integration into the new team.

## Technological and Organisational Change

At present the level of change in some organisations is unprecedented. Jobs, roles and relationships are changing as a result of:

- radical restructuring in organisations;
- changes in status of public sector bodies;
- new ways of working, due to multiskilling or teleworking.

Effective induction can help employees through these changes. It provides a delineation between old and new ways of working. With any induction scheme the aim is to ensure people are confident and motivated in their new role. Leadership is therefore vital, and the more managers and senior managers act as trainers during this process the more successful it will be.

> EXAMPLE
>
> A small publishing organisation arranged group induction training events for employees who were to be 'tele-workers', working from home. The managing director ran the programmes covering issues such as time management and workload planning. The remaining office-based staff were also taken through a programme to help them adapt to the new ways of working.

## Mergers and New Alliances

Successful alliances between organisations are the result of actions directed towards helping employees cope with the impact of different cultures. Induction must help people deal with their individual concerns for the future and the new relationships and teams in which they will be working. For these reasons induction should take place at the earliest opportunity even if some aspects of the final programme are not complete.

# Summary

*Set up induction programmes to help people as they experience significant change:*

- *Change from recruit to employee.*
- *Change from one job role to another.*
- *Change from one working pattern to another.*
- *Change from one working environment to another.*

# Evaluation of Induction Training

Evaluation measures the benefits to your organisation of induction training. It is useful to define a number of terms that are used in this context:

VALIDATING – deciding whether your induction training activities meet the objectives set.

EVALUATING – judging the benefits of induction training to your inductees and your organisation.

ASSESSMENT – determining if an induction activity enables an inductee to carry out a task, to a sufficient standard, possibly as part of a formal qualification.

The benefits from evaluating your induction training cannot be over-emphasised. Recently, the importance of evaluation has been recognised by various monitoring bodies.

### Investors in People

Investors in People is a national campaign which recognises the good business sense in investing in your people. Evaluation of training is one of the four principles on which the national Standard for Investors in People is based. Judging the value of induction training in the context of business goals is therefore an integral and ongoing part of the Standard. The value of an employee-centred approach to induction itself is recognised in the Standard through the words:

> *"An Investor in People takes action to train and develop individuals on recruitment and throughout employment.*
>
> *Action should focus on the training needs of all new recruits and continually developing and improving the skills of existing employees."*

### Quality

Quality programmes in any organisation require audits to be made of factors that affect quality. One of the elements of any quality process is training, including induction training. Evaluation of training is, therefore, an important part of any continuous improvement cycle.

### Health and Safety

Legislation that has been influenced by European Union Directives in this arena, places emphasis on proving understanding of health and safety information by inductees. This is obviously easier in organisations that systematically evaluate all aspects of their induction training.

# Evaluation of Induction Training

There are a number of levels on which you can evaluate your induction training. You can consider the effect on the individual, the team or department, and the effect on your organisation. You must also decide on the level of precision that you require from the evaluation process. Some aspects of induction training will be difficult to evaluate precisely. However, it is important to remember that evaluation should be designed as an integral part of the induction process beginning before the programme commences.

# Induction Training Objectives

The importance of defining clear objectives at the beginning of your induction process, will help focus on defined outcomes. Induction training objectives are concerned with improving or developing your inductees' knowledge, skills or behaviour. Like all training objectives, they must be:

– specific.
– measurable.
– action-orientated.
– relevant.
– time bound.

Examples of induction training activity objectives might be:

"At the end of three months, the inductees will be able to satisfy 90% of all client queries."

"At the end of the induction training programme, the inductees will be able to identify the main product areas within the organisation."

"At the end of six months, inductees will be able to transfer telephone calls to the correct department with 100% accuracy.''

# Primary Level of Evaluation (Individual)

## Reaction

The first action you can take is to find out inductees' reactions during and immediately after the training event. Discover how they are feeling and how they felt about the training. An example, during training, would be to question inductees. It could also be achieved through questionnaires or interviews, immediately after the training event or study programme. This is a measure of 'customer satisfaction', not of learning, and tests reactions to the tutor, environment and administration. It is still a valid part of the evaluation process.

## Learning

The next level of evaluation is to see what inductees have learnt. Examples of methods to evaluate learning may involve asking inductees to complete tests before, and immediately after, training events. Other ways of checking what inductees have understood may be through observing simulations or role plays, again during and following training.

## Behaviour

Learning will continue for some time after the training event. It is important, therefore, to measure the learning application a number of weeks or months after training, using a variety of methods in the work environment. This will measure the inductees' ability to *apply* their learning to their work situation. An example of this could be to observe

inductees' behaviour and performance in the work situation, before and after training. Line managers and other
staff can be involved in this process so as to improve the
quality of evaluation.

## Secondary Level of Evaluation (Organisation)

### Results

The wider level of evaluation considers the induction
training effectiveness on your department or organisation.
It is important to measure training effectiveness, so that
your organisation can decide on the level of resource
required for induction training, and whether resources are
used efficiently. Both qualitative and quantitative measures
can be used. For example attendance records, retention of

staff, flexibility of staff, inter-department liaison, customer care. By its very nature, this level of evaluation will be over a long time period. To attribute the organisational benefits totally to induction training is not possible. All that you can reasonably say is that it contributed to the results.

# Summary

| STAGE | INFORMATION SOURCES EXAMPLES | PEOPLE INVOLVED | COMMENTS |
|---|---|---|---|
| INDUCTION TRAINING OBJECTIVES | TRAINING NEEDS ANALYSIS<br><br>BUSINESS PLAN | LINE MANAGERS AND PERSONNEL AND TRAINING, AND INDUCTEES | S.M.A.R.T. OBJECTIVES |
| 1a<br><br>REACTION | QUESTION & ANSWER SESSIONS DURING AND COMMENT FORMS AT THE END OF: WORKBOOKS, COURSES, ETC. | INDUCTEES TRAINERS/ TUTORS* | DURING AND AT THE END OF THE ACTIVITY, OR IMMEDIATELY AFTER |
| 1b<br>LEARNING | TESTS TOWARDS AND AT THE END OF ACTIVITIES<br><br>TESTS SOMETIME AFTER TRAINING ACTIVITIES | TUTORS*, MANAGERS AND OTHER STAFF<br><br>MANAGERS AND OTHER STAFF | JUDGING LEARNING<br><br>JUDGING RETENTION & FURTHER LEARNING |
| 1c<br>BEHAVIOUR | OBSERVATIONS IN THE WORK SITUATION | MANAGERS, PEERS AND OTHERS | JUDGING THE APPLICATION OF LEARNING |
| 2<br>ORGANISATION<br><br>BENEFITS | AGREED CRITERIA AND BUSINESS MEASURES E.G. CUSTOMER SERVICE TARGETS, SAFETY TARGETS | SENIOR MANAGERS AND OTHER STAFF | OVER AN EXTENDED PERIOD |

*TUTOR = anyone involved directly coaching or training individual employees

## Summary of Evaluation of Induction Training

# 8

# Conclusion

Effective staff induction is the foundation of all good management practices It should be motivational, client focused and concerned to develop good attitudes as well as skills and knowledge. It is a line management function with support from specialists and others in the organisation. Induction should be structured according to employees' individual needs at various stages of their entry into a new role. Induction training programmes should be evaluated against the organisation's needs. Finally induction should be initiated whenever employees are going through significant change in their roles, their environment or their working patterns.

# Appendix 1
# Suggested Topics for Employee Handbook

## 1. Terms and Conditions

### 1.1 Hours

- normal working hours including meals and rest periods
- flexible working arrangements
- overtime or annual hours programme
- shifts

### 1.2 Pay

- frequency and method of payment

- calculation of earnings – basic wage, incentive schemes, performance related pay, commission etc.
- statutory and other deductions
- method of payment in absence
- reporting errors in payment

### 1.3 Holidays

- statutory holidays
- annual paid holidays including arrangements for part-time employees

### 1.4 Sickness Reporting Certification

### 1.5 Grievance and Disciplinary Policies and Procedures

## 2. Employee Benefits

- pension arrangements
- catering facilities
- social facilities
- welfare facilities and arrangements
- long service awards
- profit sharing and other arrangements
- housing assistance

## 3. Health, Safety and Security

- health and safety policy
- particular risks and hazards
- training in safety and fire safety
- training in prevention, measures to avoid Repetitive Strain Injury and other non-recoverable injuries
- first aid provision
- accident and emergency procedures and priorities

- employee assistance and counselling
- health promotion and fitness programmes
- alcohol and drugs policy
- smoking policy
- AIDS policy
- harassment and other threats
- dishonesty at work
- confidentiality issues

## 4. Human Resource Practice

- appraisal for employees
- training and development policy and opportunities
- open learning and other resources
- career development
- relocation policy
- induction policy

## 5. Equal Opportunities

- provision for employees with children and other dependants
- maternity provisions
- paternity leave
- adoptive leave
- access to part-time work at all levels in the organisation
- home working arrangements
- policy on employing older people
- facilities and practices for people with disabilities
- policy on employing ex-offenders

## 6. Employee Communication and Involvement

- Employee communication policy
- Team briefing and team meeting system

- Employee consultation procedures
- Union recognition
- Ideas schemes
- Range of communication channels
- Quality team membership
- Senior management forums
- House journals
- Annual report to employees

# Appendix 2
# Pre-recruitment Training

Pre-recruitment training is an employment initiative which has developed from the Industrial Society's work in inner cities. It was piloted successfully in London and South-west England in 1988 and is now running for many employers across the United Kingdom. Pre-recruitment group training courses are designed to help two groups:

- Employers who are experiencing difficulties in recruitment
- People who are experiencing difficulty in finding work.

The courses achieve this by training people looking for work in the relevant skills and knowledge required by employers with job vacancies. At the end of each course participants go through the employer's normal selection procedure.

Training topics are tailored to meet the needs of an employer, but common key elements are:

- Job related skills: literacy, numeracy, clerical, customer care, safety and sector specific skills.
- Social and personal skills: communication, teamwork, confidence building, self presentation on paper and at interview and assessment.
- Information on the employer: useful background knowledge, details on working conditions, the work environment.
- Information about the job: tasks involved, job description, hours of work.
- Interview and assessment practice.

Through pre-recruitment training employers are more able to fill vacancies particularly from people in the local community, and to benefit from the diversity of talents they bring.

# Appendix 3 Accountability Charts

GINA KING

— TONY BOLTON (Adviser)

— TREVOR BOWEN (Adviser)

— LIZ COOK (Adviser)

— JULIA SMART (Way Through Adviser)

— CLIVE WOOD (Marketing Adviser)

(Note: Names are listed in alphabetical order, irrespective of status.)

An accountability chart describes 'thick line' relationships. It shows who is accountable for the work of other staff. It is important to prepare accountability charts where ambiguity exists. Charts should be drawn up for each team in the organisation. Accountability charts complement the more complex organisation chart.

# Glossary of Induction Training Terms

## A

**ACTION CENTRED LEADERSHIP.** The model of leadership developed by John Adair based on the simple actions leaders must take.

**ACCOUNTABILITY CHART.** A chart showing the leader of a team and the people they are accountable for, listed in alphabetical order only, not according to status.

**ASSESSMENT.** A measure of whether a training activity enables a person to carry out a task, to sufficient standard, as part of a formal qualification.

## B

**'BUDDY'.** A peer, from an inductee's new team, assigned by the leader to help the inductee.

## D

**DEVELOPMENT TRAINING.** Training to promote character development and positive attitudes in young employees.

## E

**EMPLOYEE REPORT.** Employee version of the annual report.

**EVALUATION.** Measurement of the effects of training on individual employees and the organisation

## I

**INDUCTION.** Process of training to enable people to become productive in a new role in the shortest time.

**INDUCTION LOG.** Record of all training activities and achievements during induction kept by the inductee.

## J

**JOB INSTRUCTION.** A systematic process for training people in manual or simple tasks.

## M

**MENTORING.** A process undertaken by a (senior) manager to advise and guide an employee in their development.

## O

**ONE TO ONE.** A meeting drill where a manager and employee review performance and targets on a regular, often monthly, basis.

## P

**PERSONAL DEVELOPMENT PLAN.** A learner driven plan setting out targets and identifying training and development activities to achieve them.

**PRE-EMPLOYMENT.** The period between recruitment and the start of employment.

**PRE-RECRUITMENT TRAINING.** An employment initiative designed to help people looking for work, by offering
training customised to the needs of a particular employer.
At the end of the training the participants go through the
employer's normal selection procedures.

**PROGRAMMED LEARNING.** An individual training method
where an individual follows a printed or computer based
text and makes decisions on questions posed. The answers
will affect the route the employee follows through the
training material.

## R

**ROLE PLAY.** A group training method where the learner
takes on a role to test out different strategies in a 'safe'
environment.

## S

**SIMULATION.** Team based training method based on a
source document and timed interventions by a tutor.
Scenarios are played out in real time often in a competitive
environment.

## V

**VALIDATION.** Judgement of whether training activities met
the objectives set for them.

## W

**WORKBOOK.** Individual training resource, requiring open
reponses to problems and situations described.